WRITINGS ON THE WALL

Jackie Caputi

Copyright © 2018 Jackie Caputi

All rights reserved. No part of this book may be used or reproduced by any means, graphic, electronic, or mechanical, including photocopying, recording, taping or by any information storage retrieval system without the written permission of the copyright owner except in the case of brief quotations embodied in critical articles and reviews.

Making Magic Happen Academy titles may be ordered through online booksellers or by contacting:

Making Magic Happen Academy
www.makingmagichappenacademy.com

Because of the dynamic nature of the Internet, any web addresses or links contained in this book may have changed since publication and may no longer be valid. The views expressed in this work are solely those of the authors and do not necessarily reflect the views of the publisher and the publisher hereby disclaims any responsibility for them.

The intent of the author(s) is only to offer information of a general nature to help you in your quest for emotional and spiritual well-being and expression. In the event you use any of the information in this book for yourself, which is your constitutional right, the author(s) and the publisher assume no responsibility for your actions.

ISBN: 978-0-6483317-7-3 (sc)

ISBN: 978-0-6483317-8-0 (e)

Dedication

This book is dedicated to my children who
have been through so much, I love you.

It is also dedicated to the different cultures
around me that have opened my heart again,
and especially to my MEM,
you drive me crazy.

Contents

Look in front	3
Breathe in	4
Shattered	5
New day	6
Loneliness	7
Crown has broken	8
Demons	9
Narcissistic Lover	10
Long distance lovers	11
Trapped	12
Slipping away	13
Subtle art	14
Arrogance that hurts	16
Right at this moment	17
Your eyes	18
Hurts to love you	19
Sensual	20
The liquid	21
Precious cup	22
Masterpiece	23
Learnt to run	24
Crumpled paper	25

Not feeling it	26
Run away	27
Casual embraces	28
This balloon	29
Replied	30
Watching	31
Most people	32
Love hurts	33
Can I ?	34
Self-worth	35
Clichés	36
Sing me a love song	37
Self-discipline	38
Morals	39
Walk through the Forest	40
Love may call	42
Protect your heart	43
Failed dreams	44
What is love?	45
Linger	47
My angels	48
Papa	49
Waving	50

Close your eyes	52
Success	53
Monogamy	54
Words don't tell	55
Ask for more	56
My journey	57
Bachata	58
Wanted you	59
Goodnight, my love	60
Your sigh	61
Replace	62
Come into my life	63
In bed alone	64
Let go	65
He cried	66
Eternal life	68
Just you and me	69
Words no longer work	70
Nastiness	71
My age	72
God's waiting	73
On the verge	75
Life and death	76

Voyage	77
My heart told you	78
Only dreaming	80
Melancholy	81
Living a lie	82
Are you happy now?	84
All shut down	86
Salt	87
Learn	88
Vanished	90
Love to hate	91
Why bother?	92
One foot in front	93
This moment	94
Heart speaks kinder	95
Burning	96
So I sit here	98
Pretending	99
Impression	101
Someone who doesn't even know	102
No contact	104
What love is	105
Friends with benefits	107

Mind questioning why	108
Medicine	109
Silence	110
Feeling your breath	111
Cannot crumble	112
Hold my hand	113
Forever	114
Falling in love	115
Disbelief	116
The one who will hold you	117
Mumma	119
Falling apart	121
That place	122
Who am I?	123
My promise to you	124
Let go	126
This is	127
Heart in the clouds	129
Wake up to you	130
My friend	131
I want love	133
No intentions	134
Destroy	135

Blow up your sails	137
Not dating	138
Don't play with My Heart	140
Spoon	142
Rhythm	143
Before the ink runs dry	144
Superficial	146
For always	148
What would you do?	150
See me	151
Now	152
Loneliness calling	153
Inhale	154
Her crown	155
Emptiness	156
Overwhelm	157
Half full	158
About the Author	

Jackie Caputi

Look in front

When you look in front of you
And no longer behind;
When you see the happiness
And not the sorrow;
When you feel the pleasure
And not the pain,
Congratulate yourself on life's offering
And the fact that you are ready to take it...

Jackie Caputi

Breathe in

Breathe in,
Kiss deeply,
Breathe out,
Hold tightly.
Dig your nails deep into his flesh,
Let him wince in pain and delight.
Let each wave of pleasure come again
And again,
And don't stop until you have tasted
everything.
Fall asleep in his arms exhausted,
In ecstasy
And in bliss.
You are woman.
Take it all.

Shattered

Shattered on the floor like broken glass,
Fragments everywhere.
You sweep them up but still find pieces
And the splinters can cut so deep
And it hurts.
But if I become a substance that is
unable to shatter,
Then I won't be me.
Sure, I won't hurt
But I also won't feel
And while I'm alive
I want raw.
I want to feel like my insides are on the
outside,
I want my neck kissed,
I want a touch on the inside of my wrist
to make me sigh.
If that means remaining as glass,
Then that's what I shall be.
I just won't allow you to shatter me.

Jackie Caputi

New day

Each night I go to bed
saying tomorrow is a new day:
A new day to start my diet
A new day to exercise
A new day to lose 10kg
A new day to lose toxic people
A new day to find me
A new day to love myself
A new day to love my children
A new day to find my path.
My problem is that with each new day I don't start,
I remain suspended,
Waiting for a sign
That never comes,
And each new day passes,
And as the night draws upon me
I again go to bed saying...
Tomorrow is a new day

Loneliness

Loneliness is a horrible place. The feeling of EMPTINESS that takes your breath away. Sleeping so you don't have to think but then waking and nothing is solved. Everything is still the same and you don't know how to solve it. How to make things better. The lonely raindrop sitting on the leaf alone and glistening if only for a moment to then drop and completely disappear

Jackie Caputi

Crown has broken

Her crown has broken
It's tipped to the side
She tries to keep wearing it
It's broken her pride.
She reaches to adjust it
Her hand cuts against its tip
She doesn't flinch
It doesn't hurt
She feels only the trickle of blood
But there is no pain
She reaches again
And this time straightens her crown
She feels something inside her
She takes a step forward
And she may take many back
But like the crown that cut,
She will keep taking her steps

Demons

When you've unleashed your demons
And there is nowhere to contain them,
You may as well feed them
And enjoy the pleasure they bring.

Jackie Caputi

Narcissistic Lover

The narcissistic lover
Will long for you
But hold no promises;
Take you
But not keep you,
And will watch you fall
But will not reach out to stop you.

Long distance lovers

Long distance lovers
With no labels.
The emptiness of her bed
And the emptiness of his heart
Tangled together with no belonging,
When even words are forbidden
For fear they may hold a different
meaning.
So shallow conversations take place
And unanswered messages continue.
When they are together again,
Will they still be?
Or will they forever remain
Long distance lovers?

Jackie Caputi

Trapped

Trapped in her own mind
No one quite gets her
She is only at peace in her head
But when her thoughts become loud
Those around her can't quite stand the noise
They block their ears to muffle the sound
As it is too painful,
Too intense,
A sound of reasoning,
Of reckoning,
A sound not often spoken aloud
And therefore a sound not shared.

Slipping away

Slipping away,
She lost her grip.
The branch she reached for was weak
And snapped.
She held out her other hand and
reached again,
But this time there was no branch.
She was alone
And sliding downwards.
Would she hit the bottom?
What would the bottom feel like?
Maybe once she does,
She will learn to plant stronger trees

Jackie Caputi

Subtle art

The book title:
The subtle art of not giving f*ck.
Haven't read it myself
But the title lends itself to
misinterpretation,
And for those who think
Use and abuse,
F*ck and not care,
Forget it is a person,
Screw them over,
Play with their heart,
Throw them to the kerb –
I challenge you,
Look in the mirror and say out loud,
'I choose to treat others
How I want to be treated,
I choose to choose love
The way I want to be loved.
I choose to f*ck
Like there is no tomorrow
But I choose not to f*ck
With anyone's heart.'

That is ...
The subtle art of not giving a f*ck.

Jackie Caputi

Arrogance that hurts

Arrogance that hurts,
Eyes that steal,
Hands that burn.
Let yourself be misguided
And you will fall,
Fall deeply into a deadly trap,
Thinking you can change him,
Make him see what he is missing,
Make him want you more.
Let him warm your bed
But don't let him warm your heart,
Because as your heart starts to love him
He will pull away
As though you never existed.

Right at this moment

Right at this moment
I'm feeling alive
I can't sleep
I have to write
I have to let out what I'm feeling
It's magic
But if I sleep
And then I wake
Where will the magic be then?

Jackie Caputi

Your eyes

Your eyes
They've got me
They see me
And I'm scared how much they really see
But they cut through me like nothing I've felt before
Oh my God ...
Those eyes
The intensity
The sexiness
I can't look away
Because I don't want to let go of what they are giving me
Just in case the rest of you can't follow through

Hurts to love you

When it hurts to love you
But hurts even more to let you go,
When your smile drives me wild
And I feel dizzy with love,
When I want your hands all over me
And now
Don't tell me I can't have it all
Don't make me look at reality
Don't ask questions I don't want to answer
Don't let me tell you about how badly stuffed up my life really is
Just put out your f'ng arms
And love me
Because that's all I want:
You, now, no bullshit, not too much truth,
Just you

Jackie Caputi

Sensual

I feel sensual
Alive
Until she walks in the room
And the attraction of her youth
Gives my age away

The liquid

My heart is singing now
My happiness from a bottle
Bringing my senses alive
Do you know me?
The smile hiding the nerves
Lubricated by a substance
I came alive for an hour or two
And I didn't even think of you
You think you got me
But the liquid got me tonight

Jackie Caputi

Precious cup

There is a cup of kindness within my heart
And I've placed you there
I come back to this cup often
And I reunite with you
I hold you in my hands
My mouth delicately around the top
I pick you up and replace you so gently
That you do not break or spill
And you've been here for quite some time
You're so precious to me

Masterpiece

When I say your name
And breathe deeply
It's because a part of you is still with me
A part of you I may have to release
And so I breathe deeply to free you
Or most importantly, to free myself of you
So I can be a blank canvas
Awaiting the masterpiece

Jackie Caputi

Learnt to run

Energy lacking.
Where are the forces of strength?
Where is the desire to get out of bed?
Where is the willingness to succeed?
Don't let every day plague you
Like a recurring dream.
Walk alone,
Step fiercely into the unknown.
One day you will hop,
The next you will skip,
And when you begin to run, my dear,
May you outrun every horrible dream,
Every heart-wrenching pain,
Every thought of I'm not good enough,
And with your hand on your heart
May you shout out loud,
'I may be alone
And I may be lonely
But I learnt to run.'

Crumpled paper

Harden your heart,
Oh beautiful soul,
For his life is moving on.
His wheels are in motion.
He has his job,
Next will be the money
Then his search for the young beautiful bride
And you, oh beautiful soul,
Will be tossed like crumpled paper,
Discarded without a thought
But used to write upon
When there was nothing else.

Jackie Caputi

Not feeling it

Not feeling it,
Not feeling life at the moment,
Not feeling the laughter,
The warm smiles,
The little nods and winks.
I'm doing it,
But I'm just not feeling it.

Run away

Can I run away and hide?
Not forever,
Just for a few days,
But I want to come back fixed,
Repaired.
I'm tired of being broken,
Of feeling like I cannot fly.

Jackie Caputi

Casual embraces

Casual embraces,
No feelings.
How?
How do you train your body
To act without a heart?
Like drinking but not swallowing,
It's initially a relief
But it doesn't achieve anything.

This balloon

My head's about to explode,
Explode in pain,
Due to the torture of this,
This being, this life, this love
My head just won't let go
I keep telling it to,
To release the anger, the bitterness, the hate,
But it refuses and holds on even tighter.
Then I show my head a picture
Of you,
And I say 'Release!
Be this balloon,
Float away,
Exhale and go,'
And my head releases the pressure
And softens
And the torture lifts for a few moments.

Jackie Caputi

Replied

You replied...
I'd been waiting,
Not enjoying the feeling
Of waiting for a text like my heart was breaking,
But you replied
And it was simple
And it gave me the ability to sigh,
To sigh and get on with my day.

Watching

Watching a child look up at his mother,
Feeling the love and trust between
them
Like a flower and water,
Knowing what one gives to the other,
Watching closer this time
To see if the love and trust can magically
transfer to you,
So you can be both the flower and
water
And single-handedly

Learn to love and trust yourself
Once more.

Jackie Caputi

Most people

So happy for you,
With my smile on my face,
'So happy that your life is going so well'
Said with a false sense of confidence.
'No, I'm fine that you are busy
It's OK, I know life gets like that.'
I would never tell you
That to see you moving on
Makes me realise I'm standing still,
And to see you really smiling
Makes me realise my smile is false.
To hear now that you are busy
Makes me look at my empty life
And try to work out how to fill it,
Because although most people's lives
are like that,
Mine isn't,
And having had you in my life
Made me feel like most people.

Love hurts

When love walks into your life
And you grab it,
Wanting to feel it all again,
But it's not making you feel ,
It's making you hurt,
It's making each day anxious
As you wait for love to be returned,
Walking away you realise
How love is.

Jackie Caputi

Can I ?

Can I come for a coffee
So I can hear your voice,
And I can hold my cup with two hands
And feel its warmth;
So I can sit in company
And feel at peace
With some sense of belonging?
It's not what you put in my coffee
Be it whole milk or skim,
It's what you give to me
When being with you
Gives me hope and love.

Self-worth

How is it that the dependence on others becomes your self-worth?
How do you allow yourself to be given importance based on other people's actions or beliefs?
Can you love someone without really knowing them?
Can you love yourself if you don't know who you are because you have always relied on someone else to love you?
And...
When there is no someone else, you sit in mindless heartache of not knowing how to love you.
Deep questions, deep struggles with real emotions but struggling alone.
There is no one to share these things with anymore,
Everyone has gone,
Vanished from your life and your heart.
This struggle is real and it's yours
But how you wish for it to be gone,
So that you could bathe in sunlight and a happier reality alone.

Jackie Caputi

Clichés

Have you heard them before?
Clichés, sayings:
You're never too old
It can only get better
He wasn't for you
Yes I've heard them all
And they don't sit well with me
I hear myself saying them out loud to others
But I don't really believe
I'm just trying to be like the next
positive person standing next to you
Whilst the person who doesn't believe
Sits in the corner with a tear in his eye
And the inability to smile

Sing me a love song

Come sing me a love song
And take me away
To a place where there is warmth and silence,
So that I may hear your voice
And my heart will rejoice in its beauty.

Jackie Caputi

Self-discipline

Self-discipline starts now
Life choices start now
Letting love choose you
And not desperately chasing it
This time I will do it right
I will let you see
That I'm here stepping back
And you're there
Wanting me

Morals

When your guilt tells you that your
morals have dropped,
And the self-hate becomes real
Because of a wrong choice made
So you can feel desired,
And another phone rings
And it's another person wanting
To test your morals again,
Feeling desired is a wonderful thing
But living below your moral standard
can kill you.

Jackie Caputi

Walk through the Forest

Walk through the forest with me,
But do not speak.
I want to talk to those amongst the trees,
Whose eyes have watched.
I want to feel my feet amongst the leaves
That have now fallen,
I want to see how the sunlight manages
To just get through those branches,
For is not life this way...
You wish to walk but not always alone,
And you do not always need the voice of conversation.
You feel a higher sense or power around you,
Someone or something that is always watching,
And the leaves amongst your feet
Is the grounding you need.
When you touch the earth with the bareness of your body and soul
And you know that falling to the ground can be a natural process of renewing

ourselves again,
And even when life is hard the sunlight always manages to find a way through those branches.

So walk through the forest with me,
But do not speak.

Jackie Caputi

Love may call

Love may call you
But are you listening?
Is its voice real?
What is it asking of you
And how do you wish to respond?
Do you want to reply hastily
And make the wrong decision?
Or do you wish to take your time
And make the right one?
For when love calls
It may be lust,
Or it may be loneliness,
And in time when the lust has gone
Or the loneliness chose anyone to stay,
Your heart will turn to you and say,
'Love may call you
But are you listening?'

Protect your heart

Protect your heart fiercely.
Enjoy the romantic thrill of passion,
But be careful where it may take you.
On your extreme highs you can never
imagine the extreme lows,
But if you allow your heart to be taken,
Make sure it's taken slow.

Jackie Caputi

Failed dreams

Your dreams may have failed you,
Your plans not fulfilled.
Your heart has been broken
And remains broken still.
Your journey's been long
And not easy at all,
And many a time
Did you stumble and fall.
You see glimpses of hope
And shimmers of light,
And that keeps you warm
On a cold lonely night.
But you keep that light shining
And you dare to dream again,
And on a scale of one to nine
Your sadness may be ten.
New plans can be made,
New friends can be found,
New adventures and mysteries,
New sensations and sound.
Don't be afraid to start again,
However long it might take.
There is no time frame that can be put
On the new memories you make.

What is love?

When the young boy asked, 'What is love?'
Many were the replies.
Some spoke of passion, attraction,
Others of marriage, children,
Others of a unity so strong it cannot be broken.
But again the boy asked, "What is love?"
So a young girl walked towards him and held out her hand.
She said, "When you can place your hand in mine
And I feel what you feel as though it was mine,
When I want what is best for you
And you feel that way about me too,
When you can talk to me without saying a word
And I look back at you and smile because I heard,
When anger doesn't mean that we will part,
It just makes us look deeper within our own hearts,

Jackie Caputi

That, my dear boy, is love."

The boy rose to his feet, hugged her and smiled.
'Please, dear girl... hold my hand a while.'

Linger

Take that arm and wrap it around me,
Take those lips and kiss me,
Show me that wonderful gorgeous
smile,
Stay and linger for a while

Jackie Caputi

My angels

My angels on earth,
You walk beside me.
I brought you here
To love and guide me.
I feel your presence,
Your everlasting warmth.
You give me my wings
When I can no longer walk.
Your job as my guides
Will always be
To help me remember
It's OK to be me.

Papa

My papa...
You've done so much for me.
You've wept so many tears,
You've given so much strength
When I've held many fears.
I don't always know what to say
anymore
When you come and visit
And you stand at my door,
But I love you so much
And I'm sorry...
I'm sorry I'm not who I thought I'd
become;
I'm sorry my life has become so undone;
I'm sorry you've had to feel my pain;
I'm sorry you've tried to walk away.
One foot in front of the other
Is all I can say,
And I live to see another day,
And I draw on your strength
To get me through,
And I whisper at night,
'I love you.'

Jackie Caputi

Waving

When the tears begin to roll freely
And your heart begins to ache,
And you feel your body quiver
And your soul begin to shake,
Take a walk to the ocean
And find the sandiest shore,
And sit alone a while
And let the tears fall.
Imagine those tears dropping to the sand,
The sand scooping them up as if they are in his hand.
He takes them to the ocean
And deposits them there,
And whispers to the God of Sea,
'With these tears take care.'
And God of Sea takes your tears
And forms a giant wave,
And that wave meets another one,
Who tells their story of brave,
And so the waves go on meeting,
Each with something anew,
As you sit on the sand

With your tears in your hand
And the waves waving back at you.

Jackie Caputi

Close your eyes

Close your eyes, beautiful,
Rest your peaceful soul.
Awake in tomorrow's morning,
Fresh as the day is old.
Bring with it new beauty
Seen with rested eyes,
And feel the warmth against your face
As the sun lights up the skies.

Success

When your success is before you
And your book is in your hand,
When your life gives you love
But it's not as you'd planned,
Do you throw caution to the wind
And set upon life's sails
Or do you barricade yourself
Against the storm and the hails?
For you may have wished upon a different path,
And you may have stumbled in the aftermath,
But a man cannot run before he can walk
And the wise learn to listen
while the foolish will talk.

Jackie Caputi

Monogamy

Monogamy –
Just me for you
And you for me.
If that's what you want
You must show me it's true,
Just you for me and me for you.

Words don't tell

What my words don't tell you,
You will see in my eyes
When I say how I feel
And my tongue gets tied;
When the waves of emotion
Come crushing down,
When my smile disappears
And you're left with a frown;
When I write down my thoughts
And they still overwhelm,
When my heart trembles
And you're not around,
I will call out your name
And I hope you will come.
I will tell you I love you
Till you hear it as song.

Jackie Caputi

Ask for more

Deep-seated emotion,
The small sail boat
In the middle of the ocean
Feeling the many rises and falls
With my life jacket on.
Will I survive it all?

The ride will awaken you,
The swell will be great,
Your heart will be the rhythm
And love your first mate.

At the height of it all
You may come crashing down
And you may wash up on the shore,
But what can life not offer you
That you can't ask for more?

My journey

When we are alone
I'm going to take you on a journey,
A journey to my soul.
There will be winding roads,
Breathtaking views,
Bottomless pits.
I will hold your hand
And we will be blown away,
And you will look at me
And say, 'This is your soul
I never knew.'
And I will reply, 'You never asked.'

Jackie Caputi

Bachata

The Latin music
With that soulful feel,
Images of long hair In the breeze
And handsome men with amazing
smiles.
Rhythmic dancing,
Passionate beat,
Bachata.

Wanted you

I grasped the bench
With my back to it.
You walked towards me
And undressed me with your eyes.
My body was burning with desire
And you saw no one else in the room.
Your face was right in front of me,
Our lips only a breath apart.
I could feel you, hear you,
Mostly I wanted you.

Jackie Caputi

Goodnight, my love

Goodnight, my love,
Although you will never truly be,
My heart goes into a flutter when you
are alongside me.

Goodnight, my love,
May your dreams be of me
And may you wake truly wanting it to
be.

Goodnight, my love,
May our laughter soothe you,
May our hug keep you warm.

Goodnight, my love,
Wishing my heart was held by yours
And finally out of the storm.

Your sigh

When you touch your own lips in thought
And place your arm around your own waist,
And you sigh loudly simply because you can,
You realise that your lips are warm and soft,
Your waist has a gentle curve
And the sound of your sigh is beautiful.
You also realise that out of your lips come the purest of words,
Words that can cause sorrow or pain,
Happiness and laughter.
Your waist has had many embraces
And hopefully many more,
But if not
It still has the gentle curve
Of where arms once were,
And your sigh...
Oh, your sigh can say so much
Without saying a word.

Jackie Caputi

Replace

If we replace the word sex with connection
And the word kissed with love,
We could say
It is when we really love
That our connection became real.

Come into my life

Come into my life,
Sit at my table,
Drink with me.
Massage my aching shoulders,
Push aside my hair
And kiss my neck.
Carry me
When I am weary,
Love me
When I am old,
Stay and burn a light
On my soul.

Jackie Caputi

In bed alone

She lay in her bed alone,
Holding onto the memory
Of a distant lover.
Would she cry in ecstasy again,
And would the arms of a lover
Stay to soothe her aching heart?
She is too tired to search
And wants to be the strong woman alone,
But she doesn't always want her bed to be empty
And for desire to only be in her dreams.

Let go

As she walked towards him,
She was aware of her large hips,
Her wobbly thighs,
Her flabby stomach,
Her sagging breasts,
Her wrinkled skin.
He reached out his arms
And hugged her.
'It is so good to see you.'
She sighed.
Why is it we rely on someone else
For our insecurities?
Why can't we see our flaws
As beauty?
Why is it in a warm embrace
We can let go?

Jackie Caputi

He cried

You played me
To blame me,
To hurt him,
To tear us apart
Because you were jealous
Of a relationship that wasn't a relationship.
But there was something blooming
And you couldn't stand it,
So you made a plan
And you stood in our way.
You broke his heart
But he blames me,
And now my heart breaks too.
I loved him.
Yes, it was soon,
And it happened fast
And maybe we had no future,
But that wasn't your decision to make.
You did what you did out of greed,
Out of selfishness,
And he still calls you his best friend,
And he still thinks you have his best interests at heart.

And each time he talks to me now,
He tells me his life is better without me,
But I hear his heartbreak,
And I feel his pain,
And I cry the tears of wanting him.
And you played with love,
You played with two hearts, not one.
Tonight when you were not around,
He called me to say goodnight.
If we could have held each other,
We would have,
But he believes in you,
So instead
I heard him cry.

Jackie Caputi

Eternal life

Eternal life –
Eternal happiness.
When the shore rushes up to meet your feet
And when you wake with the thirst of desire,
It doesn't matter if you are partnered or alone.
Inside of you,
Deep inside of you,
Is alive

Just you and me

Could we just sit together
In my favourite place,
Listening to the waves
And watching the sea,
My head on your shoulder,
Just you and me?

Jackie Caputi

Words no longer work

When words no longer work
And action has caused harm,
When you don't believe what I say
And I hurt with your responses,
When I choose not to contact you
But my stupid self gives it one more try,
It's times like now that I wish I never felt,
I never kissed,
I never tasted.
But how sad that would be,
That because of your makeup
I would deny myself happiness,
Even if it was only fleeting.

Nastiness

Nastiness isn't inside me,
It's a bitter horrible pill
That I don't want to swallow.
That's how you choose to play your game.
Well, roll your dice,
Take your turn
And play your game alone.

Jackie Caputi

My age

At my age,
If my baggage is more like a trailer
Then those that come into my life
Better come with a tow bar.

God's waiting

When you taste your sadness
The tears start to roll,
The heat on your cheeks...

When you feel alone
But it's no different to any other day,
There is no one to share your life with...

When you try to earn a living
In a casual job
With a casual wage...

When your first attempt back at dating
Goes horribly wrong
And you fell way too early...

When you try to breathe normally
But can't control your breath...

This hasn't just begun,
This has been like this too long.

Sometimes it feels like it's just not
worth it

Jackie Caputi

But you don't know how to end.

Every day you try,
The anxiety eats you,
Love leaves you,
Hope fades you,

But every day you get out of bed,
If only for a few hours.

God's waiting.

On the verge

Never been filled with so much desire.
It's not normal,
It's a fire that can't be controlled.
Not by you,
Not by anyone.
Can this be quenched?
This thirst of sexual desire,
Awoken by a meeting.
Feeling like I'm on the verge...

Jackie Caputi

Life and death

Endless oceans,
Heart-warming sunsets,
Glasses of wine,
Friends and conversation,
Laughter and tears...
Life and death.

Voyage

Lifting myself from your clenches
I wonder what you're thinking.
Can I do it?
You bet I can.
Will I think of you?
Maybe.
Do I still want you?
Yes.
But in my mind
The journey has begun,
The voyage of discovery.
Self-pleasure is most pleasing.
No one to ask,
No one to answer.
When you hear the whispers of your name
And the tinge of sadness washes over you,
Thank you for sending me on my voyage.
Yours is yet to come.

Jackie Caputi

My heart told you

Playing with my head,
My heart told you I wanted more.
Now you think I was with someone else,
So I am the reason we are over.
Get real.
I gave it everything you allowed me to give.
I was only allowed to be half of what I could be,
But my life took more.
Your reasons were plenty
But now it's because of me.
Let me show you
Where I bleed,
Where my heart breaks
Because it wants to be loved,
Where I allowed you in
But you found a way out.
I'm lying on this floor.
Are you going to scoop me up in your arms?
Are you going to take away the pain?
Are you going to suddenly speak my language fluently?

Are you going to tell me that love will
find a way?
No, you are not going to do any of those
things,
And I am going to tell you why:
Because your arms are not strong
enough to hold a woman who has been
broken.
You cannot take away pain that you
have never felt.
My language is too complex for you
And finally, if you really wanted love to
find a way...
It would have by now.

Jackie Caputi

Only dreaming

Feeling the beauty in your eyes,
The magic in your smile,
Your hands upon my thighs...
I was only dreaming.

Melancholy

Enjoy your time,
I'll enjoy mine,
Sitting with my pillows,
Drinking white wine,
Feeling melancholy.
A new word for you,
It's basically a feeling between sadness
and blue.
So I will drink and write,
Then write some more,
My heart becoming the pages
Inside a bookstore.

Jackie Caputi

Living a lie

Living a lie,
Not a life,
Feeling empty except when I'm by your side.
There was no commitment,
No promise,
No words of hope.
My pain is all my own doing,
But my emptiness is not.
You told me you weren't ready,
You couldn't commit,
Even with me beside you,
You again chose no,
So when I stopped talking
And it hurt you,
Did you not think I was hurting too?
And when I chose to leave early,
Did you not think it was because of the pain of being alongside you?
You had your excuses,
And there were many,
But do not cry now
Because it is over.
Cry because even with all of your

excuses,
All of your reasons that didn't matter,
All of your ways of thinking that just
weren't right,
All it would have taken
Was for you to ask me to stay,
And I would have said YES!

Jackie Caputi

Are you happy now?

When you are angry
And your language isn't the best,
And you curse me
To hurt me
But don't realise what you've said,
Then you turn it around
And somehow I was the cause.
You are jealous of others
That don't even exist,
And tell me I should be beside you,
Yet clearly you were telling me not to be.
You give mixed signals
But now you are cursing,
Screaming in anger,
Saying you are going to tell others about me.
Well... about me what
You couldn't give to me
But didn't want me to walk
Until you had yelled at me through your loud hurtful talk.
Do you feel better now?
Now that you have confused me totally,

Now that I am asking what I've done
And become this wimp of a person,
Does it make you feel better to have power
And treat me like I would never treat anyone?
Do you like the fact I am sending you messages?
Does it make you feel important?
Do you get pleasure in telling someone,
'Look at what she's become'
And sniggering as though I never meant anything to you?
Does it make you feel like a man to treat me
Not like a woman?
Or does your power come from thinking you are everything,
Everything I wanted you to feel,
Everything I wanted to give,
And everything I've lost.
Yes, your anger hurts me,
Your words bruise me,
Your absence saddens me.
Are you happy now?

Jackie Caputi

All shut down

It's all shut down.
No smiles,
No ringing phones,
No texts,
No reach of your hand.
It's all shut down.

Salt

She walked towards the ocean,
The sand between her toes,
Her feet becoming wet.
She walked into the sea,
Fully clothed.
Her head below water,
She tasted the salt.

Learn

Learn to love yourself
Before loving another.
Learn to be on your own
Before complaining of being lonely.
Learn to embrace yourself
Before you ask for the arms of strangers.
Learn that although you may place others before yourself,
Others do not do the same.
Learn that life is beautiful,
Even if you spend most of it crying.
Learn that tears can wash away the hurt,
And if you cry every day, you have a lot of hurt to wash away.
Learn that you may love someone who will never love you back.
Learn that you may have the most passionate love- making with someone you cannot spend the rest of your life with;
Learn that life is not a fairy tale,
And those around you will come and go,

And when you leave this glorious earth,
Learn that you entered and exited
alone.

Jackie Caputi

Vanished

These tears that are falling,
Are they wasted on you?
This heart that is breaking,
Are you aware it's for you?
I lift my head from the pillow
But can't lift my body.
Trying to work out
How it got to this.
How did I allow my heart to be taken
By someone who didn't really care?
Now you don't call,
You don't text,
You don't look.
I've vanished from your life
And it's like I didn't exist,
And yet you've vanished from mine
But your memory is even stronger.

Love to hate

Love to hate –
So quickly do emotions turn,
Initially to protect yourself,
But then it destroys you.
Wednesday I lost you,
Your words cut me in half.
Thursday was silent,
Friday killed me,
And today, being Saturday, I cannot move.
Usually to lose someone so suddenly
Is through death,
But this wasn't death as we know it,
This was death within my soul,
Within my heart.
You didn't know I had invested so much energy in you.
You had told me from the start,
But still I loved
And still I believed.

Jackie Caputi

Why bother?

If you cannot love with all your heart,
Why bother?
If you only want to feel a little,
You're missing out.
Don't come to my heart and tap,
Only come if you are willing to knock
loudly.
Be confident in the direction you want
to take.
If the door is open,
You may enter gently,
But once you are in,
Throw caution to the wind
And feel everything.
Wear your heart out loud,
Kiss every inch of me,
Make my body arch,
And tell my soul you're coming in.

One foot in front

Put one foot in front of the other
And climb a little higher.
Smile at the next person you see,
Even when you feel like crying.
Give in love and in life.
Give not so that you can receive,
But because you can.

Jackie Caputi

This moment

Place your head on my lap,
Let your worries drift away.
Stop thinking of tomorrow
Or re-living your yesterday.
Be with me for this moment.
Be at peace with your soul.

Heart speaks kinder

I saw you today.
I held your hand,
I kissed you,
I made love to you.
I also heard you;
I heard you say yet again how we can't be.
I heard you say you don't want to get too attached.
I also saw you;
I saw the way you looked at me
When I casually looked away.
I saw the way you held my glance and didn't want to look away.
Why is it that
Your words say hurtful things,
But your heart speaks kinder?

Jackie Caputi

Burning

God Damn crazy,
Crazy for you,
Can't think of anything else
Except when I can be with you.
Trying to act normal
Like I don't need you around,
Trying to convince myself
That this is not happening.
Then you phone,
I hear your voice,
My heart skips a beat
And I try to act again.
But when I actually see you
I want you longer than you can give,
And I want you more than I say,
But I can't give up my act
Because that will give it all away.
And what if you do want me,
And how will I cope with that?
What if your heart beats too,
And what if I give it back?
We started playing with fire,
Not thinking we would get burnt,
But as the flames grew bigger

The heat took over,
And we allowed it to,
Thinking we were stronger
And thinking we could pull away.
So whilst the fire has engulfed us both
And we keep it ignited,
Thinking that we were OK,
The flame is burning brightly in my heart
And I'm holding my hand over it
So you can't see the flame.
But who am I kidding?
You've seen through it,
You've felt the heat,
And you've commented on the beauty
of the flame
As we both sat together BURNING.

Jackie Caputi

So I sit here

So I sit here all alone,
With no one beside me but my phone.
I think of you and want to call
But I'm not sure I could cope with it all.
So I sit here all alone,
Picturing your face,
And I think of how you looked at me,
And I kiss your memory.
I hold on to our words,
I remember our laughter.
We held each other so tight
As we laughed so hard we almost cried.
But I sit here all alone,
With no one beside me but my phone.
I think of you and want to call,
But I'm not sure I could cope with it all.

Pretending

Pretending it is more,
Feeling what I want you to feel.
Your words convey less than your eyes;
Your eyes tell me more,
Your hands constantly reaching for mine.
But when you speak,
And you speak of the life you want to live,
The life that doesn't even hint that I am in it,
That's when my heart aches.
That's when I tell myself to listen.
But yet again you look at me,
And your eyes say the words I want to hear,
And your hands touch me in a way that says this is not casual,
And your lips kiss like you want to kiss me forever.
So for now stop speaking,
And listen to the unspoken words you are telling me,
Then ask yourself 'Can I live without

Jackie Caputi

her,
And can I love like this?
Or am I letting my belief tell me who
and how to love?
Am I letting this real love slip away?'
Because what we have is real
But you are pretending it's not
And I am pretending it is.
Let's be real.
Let's do this.

Impression

It is within my heart
That this feeling comes.
It is within my soul
That I want to burn.
It is within my mind
That I want you to think;
To feel like you have never felt;
Touch like you have never touched;
To leave an impression
On your heart,
Your soul,
Your life.

Jackie Caputi

Someone who doesn't even know

Why do I keep looking at you,
Wanting you?
Why do you lure me
But not really want me?
Why have I forgotten my age,
And feel so helpless?
Why do I keep walking back,
Then listen to you desiring others?
Why is this friendship not enough for me?
Why do I want you as my lover?
What if I had you as a lover?
Then I would still want you as my partner.
I want you to tell others about us.
Why do I feel this way?
Why can I still taste your kiss
But can't kiss you again?
Why does your scent drive me wild?
Why do your eyes pierce deep into my heart,
My soul lay open,
And I feel so lost,

Lost in love,
In love with someone who doesn't even know?

Jackie Caputi

No contact

So today I'm going no contact
But sent a message by nine,
Had a quick response,
I had you on the line.
Didn't message again,
Although I will see you tonight;
Not to hold you or love you,
But because I have to be there
With other commitments...
So I'm not going to chatter,
I'm not going to fumble.
I'm going to see you,
Acknowledge you,
And continue on with my task.
Now if you want my heart again,
You will have to ask.

What love is

Each day got longer,
More intimate,
Hands held,
Kisses exchanged,
Bodies touched.
Each day she got closer,
Closer to telling him she loved him.
The obstacles felt too great,
She didn't want to acknowledge it.
Right at the height of their love
He turned to her and said,
'This cannot be.
I want children,
I want something else
With someone else.
I love you,
But we can't be...'
She held his hand,
Kissed his lips,
And slowly walked away.
He reached out for her
And she turned to him and said,
'Hold onto my heart,
But only if you intend to hold it tightly,

Jackie Caputi

To love me,
Respect me,
And want for nothing else.
Because what my heart will give you
Is all the things you want
When you realise what love is.'

Friends with benefits

So you're busy...
Yep, busy,
Too busy to talk,
Too busy to see me.
What were we?
Nothing but friends with benefits?
Initially that starts with friends,
But how quickly that means nothing
When the benefits are gone.
You creep!
I feel so angry,
So hurt,
And yet I knew all along.
You can keep your 'friends with benefits'.
I don't want it.
I don't want you.
You couldn't care less
And you played the game so well.
Goodbye my little whatever you are.
You're not playing me anymore
Because I've finished the game
And I'm not keeping score.

Jackie Caputi

Mind questioning why

You can't make someone love you.
I'm sitting here watching and waiting,
Feeling so much for you,
And you are there, still feeling for her
And telling me all about it.
Goddamn you!
Open your f'ng eyes,
Look at me!
What more can I say?
What more can I do?
This is killing me.
I'll walk away
And you will ask why.
You tell me all the time that this can't work.
They're your words,
Not your heart,
So watch what happens when I walk.
Watch your heart crumble
And then listen to your mind asking 'Why?'

Medicine

What did you call me?
The medicine your body is rejecting?
You've been hurt before -
So have I and even more.
I come with baggage
And so do you.
I wish to share some happiness,
To share some love.
Feel good when I'm with you
And not so good when we're apart.
Without you even realising,
You're helping to mend my broken
heart.

Jackie Caputi

Silence

Silence at the end of a phone call,
Not knowing what to say.
Too early to say 'I love you'
But I don't want you to walk away.
Hesitating before the kiss,
Nervous after an embrace,
Texting in a moment of confidence,
Images of your beautiful face.
Let's be together,
Throw out what it's meant to be.
Let's be together,
Together, just you and me.

Feeling your breath

Feeling your breath,
Watching you rise,
Wanting you to love me
So desperately.
Anxious feelings,
My hands on you
Constantly.
So hard to stop myself.
Why do I want you so bad?
Is it because you don't want me?
Do we have anything in common?
I don't know.
It's been such a long time alone.
But stand beside me again,
And again I will have to touch you.
My desire is great,
Not only for touch
But for love.
Will you love me?

Jackie Caputi

Cannot crumble

When your breathing becomes difficult
And you gasp for more air;
When the ground at your feet
Is no longer there;
When you reach for a hand
And there is no one around;
When your world becomes one
That is empty of sound,
So hard to keep going.
So difficult to explain
Why you can't solve your problems,
Why you stay in this pain.
It's not what you're choosing
And not what you want,
But it is what it is
And it's hard to move on.
Keep pushing forward,
Keep looking for that light.
You cannot break again,
You cannot crumble tonight.

Hold my hand

Are you nervous to hold my hand?
Are you worried what it could mean?
It means we've connected
And we're comfortable with it,
But I can see you pull back.
You reach out but then, not sure.
It's OK,
I don't bite.
I want to hold your hand,
I want to sit with that feeling of
Yep... I'm with him,
We're together.
It will be weird
And scary when someone we know
sees,
But it feels great at the same time.
Let me hold your hand.

Jackie Caputi

Forever

She lay in his bed.
He asked if she would like him to join her.
She replied with a yes,
To which he came in,
He lay beside her,
Looked in her eyes
And drew her towards him.
He kissed her slowly,
His eyes not moving from hers.
He smiled at her.
She smiled back.
She leant forward to kiss him again.
Each kiss was returned.
He was so gentle,
Soft and slow.
She felt like she had known him forever.
He touched her
And loved her,
And she melted into his arms.

Falling in love

Can't fight this feeling
And I'm not going to.
I know what's going on
Between me and you.
I've seen it in your eyes,
Your actions tell me too,
There's something going on
Between me and you.
Your messages tell me how you feel.
When I see you
It's difficult to pretend,
But when we're alone
We are more than friends.
I've fallen for you
And you for me, too.
I hate to say it out loud
But I think I'm falling in love with you.

Jackie Caputi

Disbelief

Don't look at me in disbelief.
You are the one who walked away,
You are the one who tore out my heart
And ripped out my soul.
Don't look at me now and wonder,
Wonder what happened to me.
I was destroyed,
I was emotionally suffocated.
I'm clinging to the very part of life
That keeps on,
Trying to support our children,
Showing them that love is still around them.
Trying to show them that although I see them less,
I love them more;
Trying to tell them that although life is difficult,
It won't always be;
Trying to explain that my heart is trying to repair the damage that you have done.
My life path is blurred
But I cling to the hope of happiness.

The one who will hold you

Love the One who will hold you
When everyone else walked away.
Love the One who holds your hand
And asks if he can stay.
Love the One who looks at you
And sees the person, not the object;
And when you feel rejected because of
the lack of desire,
Love the One who wants to be your
friend.
He doesn't want a lover,
He wants a best friend.
He wants to sit and talk,
He wants to hold your hand and keep it
warm.
He promises adventures,
He talks of travels together.
His future isn't with you as his partner,
But it is with you as a part of his life.
It may be a small part,
It may be a large part,
But it is a part,
And he loves you
As a friend,

Jackie Caputi

And for that
You should love him too.

Mumma

Wish you were here.
I really need you.
I go to pick up the phone,
Or drive to your house;
Long to see your face
Or smell your perfume.
And I remember you're not here,
I remember you left
As I lay by your bedside
Watching you slip away.
The years have gone by
And now I miss you more.
I ache for not feeling more when you were alive.
I wish I had told you how much I loved you
Instead of waiting to tell you every day when you were sick.
Why didn't I tell you when you were healthy?
And now each day that my mind is unwell
I only want you;
To see you again, Mum,

Jackie Caputi

To hug you so tight,
To tell you I love you,
And to hear you tell me everything is
going to be all right.
I wish you were still here, Mumma.
I miss you more than words can ever
say,
More than I ever imagined,
And it seems to grow stronger each day.

Falling apart

Not sure what I'm feeling,
Want to be there for myself.
Can't shift my downward spiral,
It's sucking me in.
Feeling hopeless in my pull downwards,
Keeping that false smile,
False positivity,
But inside I'm drowning.
Want more from my life,
Falling apart.

Jackie Caputi

That place

I'd like to lie and just look at you.
I'd like to lie in your arms,
Caressing you,
Touching your face,
Stroking your hair,
Not saying a word,
Lingering with feelings.
Then slowly take you,
First by kissing your mouth,
Gently touching your lips.
Then my hand sliding down your chest,
My heart racing,
My head dizzy,
My breath short.
I'd like to take you to a place
Where your body spasms,
Where you moan in ecstasy,
Where you lie breathless afterwards,
Where your heart beats loudly.

I'd like to take you to that place.

Who am I?

Who am I?
I'm a mother,
I'm a daughter,
I'm a sister,
I'm a friend,
I'm a lover,
I'm a worker.
All these identities...
Who am I?

I'm lost.

Jackie Caputi

My promise to you

I love you,
I really do.
I'm trying so hard to stay here with you,
To be the best that I can,
So that I can give you the best,
The best you deserve.
I'm trying so hard to be normal,
To act normal,
To think normal.
I'm not sure how to do it,
How to survive,
How to work,
How to live,
How to be happy.
But that is one thing I so desperately
want to be:
Happy.
Not in a false sense,
With a false set of friends,
A false set of lovers,
But back to real,
My family being happy and thriving,
My smile being genuine,
My children's arms wanting to be

wrapped around me,
And me wanting to give.
People think I'm not trying.
If only they were in my mind,
If only they could help me wipe the pain away,
If they could give my children back the mother I once was.
And to my children...
I'm still here,
I still love you.
I'm trying so hard to get out of the fog,
The fog that has turned your lives to misery in the past few years.
I'm trying so hard to turn it around.
I don't want to see each of you in pain anymore.
It kills me even more inside,
And every day I tell myself today is the day,
The day of change.
I want to take away your pain,
And I will,
I promise you that.

Jackie Caputi

Let go

It's come to this:
Empty, but not completely broken.
I want you to go away now,
Leave me as I am,
Alone.
Leave me how you found me.
I will get there,
Not on my own forever.
You think you can break me,
Well I can't go lower than I am,
So don't sit and wait,
Just walk away and leave.
You served a purpose.
Now I have to let go of attachment,
Let go of any feeling,
Let go of fairy tale stupidity,
Let go of you,
Let go.

This is

When you feel like giving up
But something holds you back;
When you feel like leaving
But something makes you stay;
When there's no One there to love
But you think there may be one day,
And when each day is killing you slowly:
Remember, tomorrow is another day.
The light may shine brighter.
Remember that love can be overrated.
Relationships end.
You don't need anyone except yourself,
And when yourself is defeated
And beaten up to the last breath,
Somewhere there is more wind beneath you.
Don't give up just yet.
If you can't get help,
And you can't get love,
Put your arms around yourself,
Sit and hug.
Hug as though you are all there is in this world,
Hug like there is no tomorrow.

Jackie Caputi

Bring comfort to yourself.
It has to get easier.
It has to get better.
You cannot continue to live like this
Because this is not living,
This is not even existing.
This is.

Heart in the clouds

Stirring emotions,
Desire going crazy.
Can't satisfy it yet.
One day I will be fulfilled,
And every aching part of me will feel satisfied.
The throbbing will have been tasted,
And seduction taken to every level.
I will walk with feet on the ground,
But heart in the clouds.

Jackie Caputi

Wake up to you

It's time to close your eyes,
Switch off from the day,
Lie in bliss
And dream away.
I look forward to the night
Where for a few hours everything stops,
And if I'm lucky I can dream,
Dream of brighter days,
Bigger hearts,
Warmer smiles;
Dream of love and passion,
Dream of my new life,
And when I wake,
I wake up to you.

My friend

Can I help you, my friend,
When I can't help myself?
You don't know everything about me
And there are things I just can't tell you yet,
And maybe I never will.
I want to be there for you,
I want to see what can grow,
But can we start in reverse?
We were intimate first,
And now we are just friends.
I'm hoping it will develop into something more
But I cannot push it
Or it will push you away,
And I can't be honest and open
As there are some secrets that have to remain.
I have parts of my life I just can't share,
But I want to share myself with you.
How will I do this?
How will I create warmth in our hearts?
I'm not sure yet,
And don't know when I will be.

Jackie Caputi

Meanwhile I will tiptoe beside you
And see what develops from there.

I want love

I want love.
I want to be in someone's arms
That will never let me go,
And never want to.
I want to feel safe again,
To feel never alone.
I want to be wanted,
I want to be looked at like I am 21 again.
I want love.

Jackie Caputi

No intentions

She walked into the store
And you looked at her, and then looked some more.
You made a joke,
You gave me a smile,
You thought it was funny
I cared about you.
I was there,
I listened and believed that we had something.
All around me laughed as I was another one,
Another one that you had taken.
You kept reeling me back in,
Telling me after your plans we could have something.
You have no intention of that at all.
You just like the feeling of being someone's something
So you can tell people to have a laugh at my expense.
If you ever achieve your plan,
You will simply wave goodbye
And not care that you took my heart with you.

Destroy

I felt it tonight,
I felt you pull away.
I felt what has been building up these
past few days.
Our time has come,
We're over, we're through,
Our fun has ended
And I'm nothing more to you.
I was kidding myself
To think that I was more,
To think we could really be something
And that you would look at me
differently.
But the game is over,
You're already checking out who's next
Or possibly who is already,
And the feeling that I was special
Has become a feeling of 'I am
worthless',
Another number to add to your belt.
And I look at myself as stupid,
Stupid for allowing you to alter who I
am,

Jackie Caputi

Who I was
And what I stood for.
I allowed moments of pleasure
To destroy my soul,
My hope,
My credibility;
To destroy me.

Blow up your sails

Come away with me,
Come blow up your sails
And set me free.
Come sail those oceans,
That deep blue sea,
Where its depth is unknown
And its rage is wild.
It cannot be tamed,
It cannot be guessed.
Let's do it anyhow,
Let's do it now.
If you're not ready,
I'll do it alone.
I'll sail those oceans,
I'll discover new shores,
I'll feel some things I've never felt
before.
I'll only ask you once more:
Come away with me,
Come blow up your sails
And set me free.

Jackie Caputi

Not dating

We're not dating,
We're just...just what?
You're playing me,
No, I'm playing you.
Are we exclusive?
Of course not.
Do I feel guilty?
Hell, yes.
Do you?
I doubt it.
Dating today,
No, this isn't dating,
This is a game,
A sad horrible game
Where we fulfil our desire
And walk away
With not one, not two,
With as many as you can do.
Sometimes the desire isn't even fulfilled,
We just keep trying.
That fulfilment will never come,
Not after you,
Not after him,
Or him.
There's nothing there,
Nothing here.

Stop searching...

Damn!

Jackie Caputi

Don't play with My Heart

Your culture is different,
Your age is too young,
I'm at the end,
You haven't begun.
I've tasted you
And wanted more,
But walked away
And out the door.

You've crept back in
To linger, to tease,
To do whatever it is you please.

I'll hold you,
I'll love you,
But watch my heart...

It's been broken, it's fragile,
It can mend in your hands,
Drop it again and It will explode

Fragments of my heart will pierce your hands,
Reminding you that...

Hearts aren't made to be played with.

Especially mine.

Jackie Caputi

Spoon

Spoon beside me,
Let me lie in your arms.
I just want to feel safe one more time,
To feel your chest against my back,
To arch so you can kiss my neck,
To feel your knees up against the back
of mine.
Let me fall asleep like this forever,
Telling me you love me
As the weight of my day disappears,
And nothing else matters,
Nothing except you and me
And the way you are holding me right
now.

Rhythm

Can you hear that?
'Hear what?' she replied
The beating of my heart.
'Yes, its rhythm matches mine'

Place your hand on my heart,
Now close your ears
And feel the rhythm.
Can you feel that?
'Yes, its rhythm matches mine.'
Kiss me.
What did you hear?
Kiss me.
What did you feel?
Kiss me again.
Your rhythm matches mine.

Jackie Caputi

Before the ink runs dry

Words –
My head is filled with them.
I can't stop,
My mind wants to be satisfied.
I write them down
Hoping you will read them,
Hoping someone will hear my yearning,
My yearning to be heard,
To be understood,
To be loved,
To be cherished.

Alas, to write as though that is all there is.

There is nothing else
To allow you to feel my heart trying to explode,
Trying to explain

I'm going to burst,
Burst with love,
Passion,
Nerves,

Adrenaline.

At this stage it is only by my words am I able to express it.
Even then, its expression isn't enough.

Come with me,
Make my words come alive.

Live my words before the ink runs dry.
Live with me.

Jackie Caputi

Superficial

You look so beautiful
In your designer jeans
And your well-styled hair.

You look so beautiful
With your manicured nails
And your perfect smile.

You look so beautiful
With that perfect body
And glowing skin.

But...

Your designer jeans won't always look
that good,
Your well-styled hair will grey,
Your manicured nails will be on wrinkled
hands,
Your perfect smile won't shine so bright,
Your perfect body won't be perfect
And your glowing skin won't glow.

It is then that you will know

I love you,
I love you for the inner you,
I love you for what is in your heart

What time has taught me about you is
what I love.
Time will take away the superficiality
And time will show you

I loved you then,
I love you now,
And I will love you

Always…

Jackie Caputi

For always

How can something that feels so right
be so wrong?
How can something that allows you to
feel again be not OK?
Why is age appropriate and
inappropriate?
Why do your plans in life have to be in
concrete?
Why can't you move to allow me in?
Why do you want to feel but not keep?
Why do you want to tease yet feel
love?

How do you think you can keep this
going?
How does your heart not say stop?
How does your conscience let you
continue
When you know...

She is falling,
She is feeling,
She is loving,
She is trembling with desire;

Desire to have you,
To hold you,
To feel you,
To touch you;
Desire to hold on and not let go,
Desire to love,
To connect,
To enmesh,
To be wrapped in your arms,
To feel safe,
Wanted,
Loved,
Not only for today,
Not only for this moment,
Not only for this hour,
Not only for this week,
But...

For always.

Jackie Caputi

What would you do?

What would you do if you could stop the pain,
If you could stop the senseless mind fuck
That is life?

What would you do if you could wake up
To a beautiful day,
To a life worth living,
To a heart worth loving?

What would you do?

You would do.

See me

Hold my hand,
Stroke my hair,
Look into my eyes
And know I'm really there…
I'm not just the empty soul
You see,
I'm aching for love.
I'm learning to love myself
So that you can love me,
And if not you, then I will have the strength,
I will have the strength to only let in the one who deserves me the most.
The one who looks at me like there is no one else.
The one who sees me beyond
My age,
My children,
My ageing body,
My greying hair,
My life,

The one who sees ME.

Jackie Caputi

Now

Don't hold my hand to let it go,
Don't touch my soul to watch it glow,
Don't be the burden in my heart,
Don't walk away and never start.
Be the fire to start the spark,
Be the passion in my heart,
Hold me like you'll never let me go
And don't just stop to say hello.
Linger in the feeling,
Stay long enough to feel your heart warm.
Sit with those feelings,
Don't be scared to feel something.
It can't be perfect.
My life is not that way.
It can be the new kind of life,
To live with me each day.
Feel it,
Touch it,
Taste it,
Want it,
Now.

Loneliness calling

Peace has come to me tonight.
Anxiety is resting,
Love stopped by to say hello,
Flirting was in sight,
Disappointment stepped in briefly,
Self-esteem took a step sideways,
Desire made a brief appearance
But only because loneliness was calling
its name.

Jackie Caputi

Inhale

I heard your breath,
I inhaled it.
As you smiled,
I watched your lips curl.
I knew that your next gesture,
Was to shake your head
And as you did so,
To say my name.
I waited in silence on the phone,
Just because you were on the other end.
I sleep,
Hoping I will see you tomorrow
But if I don't....
Thank you for what you gave me today.

Her crown

Her crown has broken,
It's tipped to the side.
She tries to keep wearing it,
It's broken her pride.
She reaches to adjust it.
Her hand cuts against its tip.
She doesn't flinch,
It doesn't hurt,
She feels only the trickle of blood
But there is no pain.
She reaches again,
And this time straightens her crown.
She feels something inside her,
She takes a step forward
And she may take many back,
But like the crown that cut,
So too will she keep taking steps.

Jackie Caputi

Emptiness

As I sit here thinking, what can I do?
I sit here thinking of each of you.
I brought you into this world but feel
like I've let you down.
I want to talk to you,
I want to reach out.
I love you,
I'll never say goodbye.
I just wish I had more to offer you,
More than my fake smile,
My broken heart,
My dreams with no foundation,
My EMPTINESS.

Overwhelm

Satisfaction.
Wanting companionship.
How to do it all?
Want to do nothing but everything all at once.
Nothing gets done,
Nothing.
That's not a lie,
It's truth.
Day 1 to day 365,
They're all the same,
And who is beside you?
You.

Jackie Caputi

Half full

You don't know me but you're going to.
I'm the one inside of you.
I make you tick.
I'm your heart,
Your soul.
You've used and abused me
But I'm still going...
You've wondered if you're still alive,
You've been paralysed by fear.
You are still alive and one day soon
you'll feel it,
Feel it in your body,
Feel it in your eyes.
You will look in the mirror and start to
remember who you are,
You will look past the mirror and start to
plan your future.
You won't always feel this way.
One day the glass is half empty,
The next it is half full.

About the Author
Jackie Caputi

Jackie Caputi lives in Perth, WA. She is a single mum to four children. She has had many struggles in life but has always dreamt about inspiring others through her words.

This is her debut poetry collection.

Jackie truly hopes that you enjoy it.

You can find Jackie on Facebook

https://www.facebook.com/Writings-On-The-Wall-1993569904263982/

www.ingramcontent.com/pod-product-compliance
Lightning Source LLC
Chambersburg PA
CBHW071926290426
44110CB00013B/1498